Fear, Anger & Boxing

Mastering the Mind and Body

Gavin O'Reilly

© 2023 Gavin O'Reilly. All rights reserved.

Dedicated to all the Boxers and Coaches of Crumlin Boxing Club.

About the Author

Gavin O'Reilly is an accomplished writer in the realms of geopolitics and globalism, being published on multiple outlets around the world since 2017. In his first foray into the literary world, he follows his other passion - health & fitness. His debut book *Fear, Anger & Boxing - Mastering the Mind and Body* explains the role of the body's fight or flight system and how the sport of Boxing can bring it under control. Clear and concise, this book explains with brevity lessons that will last a lifetime on mental fortitude, self-confidence and discipline.

Table of Contents

Introduction
7

Fear
10

Anger
35

Boxing
49

Conclusion
57

Introduction

It was Summer 2007, when having previously trained in martial arts, I first discovered not just my love of Boxing, but also an interest in the concept of controlling fear, sparked by an online post on Bebo (the most popular social media outlet for young people at the time) of an interview with Kevin Rooney, former trainer to Mike Tyson, outlining his mentor Cus D'Amato's approach to fear; rather than to let it paralyse you, to use it as intended, a highly-effective fuel that gives you a physical and mental edge in times of danger. To me, this was a life-changing concept.

Pursuing my newfound interest in Boxing, I joined my local club, which happened to be the world famous School of Excellence, Crumlin Boxing Club - home of none other than the Notorious Conor McGregor.

Training hard for several years and competing on a number of club shows, I developed myself both physically and mentally, learning crucial lessons about life that I still apply to this day.

My interest in fear and how to control it continued, and in recent years this led me to begin researching Anger also. I realised that both emotions are ultimately two sides of the same coin, the fight or flight response, and that it is crucial that we learn to control both.

You can be fully-aware of the role of anger, but should you lack the same understanding of fear, you may be left unable to adequately confront whatever, or whoever, causes your anger in the first place, ultimately allowing it to simmer.

Likewise, you can be fully-aware of the role of fear, but a lack of understanding towards anger means that rather than shying away from necessary confrontations, you instead respond in a disproportionate manner, exploding at the smallest slight. This brings about its own problems.

The sport of Boxing is one that allows you to simultaneously gain control of both emotions, and through this book I will explain how. It is important to note however, that merely reading this book alone will not bring about change in your life, the lessons learned from it have to be applied on a daily basis for that to occur. The fact you are reading it in the first place however, shows that you have already taken the first step.

Let us begin.

FEAR

What is Fear?

What is fear you ask? To put it simply, fear, essentially, is an energy. An energy with an intended purpose.

Imagine your caveman ancestor walking through a forest. Though initially relaxed as he searches for Berries and other foodstuffs, his senses are quickly alerted by the nearby sound of a branch crackling and leaves rustling.

Turning around to discover the source of these sounds, he's greeted by the sight of a Sabre Tooth Tiger; a magnificent beast that could tear him asunder with ease, and as a Carnivore, fully intends to do so.

A huge amount of adrenaline is automatically released into your ancestor's bloodstream, and all conscious thought is suspended, instead replaced with an instinctual focus on removing himself from this situation as quickly as possible, his life on the line if he fails in this task.

Fortunately though, he does manage to escape, with the adrenaline released giving him the energy to run faster and for longer than in his initial relaxed state. His mental state, initially at ease as he walked through the forest, immediately switched to a more focused version, quickly allowing him to determine the most effective escape route from the predator, thus allowing him to survive and eventually reproduce - with you being born generations later as a result.

Now, let's imagine a similar situation in a more modern context.

It's a beautiful Summer's day and you're walking down the street on the way to meet friends. Children are out playing in gardens, music is playing from passing cars and elderly people smile at you as they pass by.

In a relaxed state and taking in the sights and sounds of the day, your attention is then suddenly drawn to the louder than usual revving sound of a nearby car.

Turning around to investigate further, you're greeted by the sight of a 2.6 litre gas guzzler - its owner having suffered sun stroke and lost control - veering in a straight line in your direction.

Just as in the situation with your ancestor and the Sabre Tooth Tiger, a rush of adrenaline immediately surges through your veins. Your mental state, initially relaxed as you enjoyed the day, instantly switches to a state of intense focus, which, combined with the sudden burst of energy, results in you making the split-second decision to jump over a nearby wall – one that takes the full brunt of the car rather than your legs, with the driver thankfully surviving without injury due to his seatbelt and the release of the car's airbag.

Just like your ancestor in the forest millennia beforehand, fear - a component of the mind and body's fight or flight system - served its purpose by preparing you physically and mentally to escape from an immediate threat to your life, in this case an out of control car, and in your ancestor's, a carnivorous predator, with both situations sharing the same common factor of fear acting as a survival mechanism, thus preventing serious injury or death.

Is Fear a good thing then?

To put it simply, yes.

In both situations described, fear acted as an energy source that fuelled an escape from certain injury or death; and I'm certain that as you read through them, your mind was brought back to real-life situations you experienced where your fight or flight system acted in a similar manner e.g. similar to the situation with the car, you perhaps once strolled across what you thought was a quiet road without checking for traffic, only to instinctually run across when you were alerted to an oncoming car, thus avoiding being knocked down.

In short, fear is what has guaranteed the survival of humanity for generations, and should be recognised for being the real-life super power that it effectively is.

What **IS** a bad thing however, is the mismanagement of fear.

What is the mismanagement of fear?

As already mentioned, fear is an energy source, one that has likely ensured your survival in many situations throughout your life, where a genuine risk was present.

The mismanagement of fear however, leads us to perceiving threats in situations where there is none, preventing us from doing things that we **WANT**, **SHOULD** or **NEED** to do.

As the legendary Boxing trainer Cus D'Amato once said

"Fear is the greatest obstacle to learning. But fear is your best friend. Fear is like fire. If you learn to control it, you let it work for you. If you don't learn to control it, it'll destroy you and everything around you."

As has already been stated, fear is ultimately a form of energy, and energy cannot be created or destroyed, only converted.

In a genuinely dangerous situation, fear is converted into the fuel that is necessary to escape certain injury or death.

In the modern era, we are not faced with the threat of Sabre Tooth Tigers. Nevertheless, the fight or flight system continues to operate as intended, with it being important to note that

the brain cannot differentiate between a physical and mental threat.

Picture the scene, after months of job hunting, you've landed an interview with a firm you've aspired to work for for a long time, in a role that you've sought after.

Come the morning of the interview, your mind immediately focuses on what will happen if you don't land the job. Will you suffer stress as a result of your financial situation? Will you have to settle for a job you despise to make ends meet?

Despite there being no threat to your physical wellbeing, a slight unease begins to set in, such as the infamous 'butterflies in your stomach'.

The first thing to note is that this is a completely normal reaction.

Your brain has determined that there is a potential threat present and as a result, is preparing you physically and mentally to deal with said threat.

Though uncomfortable, you soldier on through it, sailing through the interview with flying colours.

Once over, though you're consciously aware that you should feel more calm, you still feel on edge physically and mentally. Again this is a biological throwback to our hunter-gatherer days, when although we may have escaped from a dangerous predator, we had to still be on alert that the location we escaped to didn't have yet another dangerous predator residing in it.

Half an hour passes before you calm down completely, with you wondering to yourself why you were so worked up about the interview in the first place. You laugh about it, with the feeling of apprehension soon replaced with one of elation when you receive a phone call asking are you available to start the job on Monday.

Ultimately, this is the healthiest attitude to have towards fear, to **face it head on and not let it fester**, and through this book, is one I hope to cultivate in all of its readers.

The mental aspects of fear

Though the physical aspects of fear are well-documented, the mental side is less so, with many mistakenly believing it is a fully physical phenomenon.

To control fear, we must understand it, and to understand it, we must go to where it begins — in the mind.

As has been mentioned, the activation of the fight or flight system is never a conscious decision. Subconsciously, our mind has determined that someone or something is a threat, and whether justified in this classification or not, it is ultimately our responsibility to manage this response.

Going back to the example of your caveman ancestor, it was necessary for his survival to focus only on the immediate threat of the predator in his midst. Had he not paid attention and been distracted by nearby leaves and Berries, he would likely not have survived the encounter and you would not be reading this book right now.

This is ultimately the basis for why human beings worry. Our fight or flight system has detected a potential threat to our physical or mental wellbeing, and it has mentally honed in on it in order to determine the best course of action, with our brain regarding focusing on anything else as being detrimental to our survival.

It is also why we usually imagine the worst possible situation that could happen; this is our brain's way of predicting potential future developments from perceived threats and how to deal with them.

On this piece of information it is very important to note that **THE WORST POSSIBLE THING THAT CAN HAPPEN IS VERY RARELY THE LIKELIEST THING THAT WILL HAPPEN.**

Again this is a survival instinct intended to help us prepare for future threats.

It is also an essential reason as to why we need to face our fears head on, lest the energy produced manifests itself as needless worry and anxiety.

The physical aspects of fear

The physical aspects of fear are well-known, the biological reasons for these aspects, not so much. In order to manage fear in a healthy manner, it is necessary to understand why our body responds in a certain way to this powerful emotion.

What is perhaps the most well-known physical aspect of fear is an increased heartbeat - this is necessary to quickly pump adrenaline throughout our body in order to give us the energy needed to escape from danger.

As a result of this, our muscle's temperature quickly rises, leading us to sweat more in order to cool them down. Hence, why excessive sweating is associated with nervousness.

Next, our brain sends a signal to our stomach to slow down digestion, with this being seen as a non-essential method to escape and the energy it uses being diverted towards fleeing instead. This is where the saying 'Butterflies in the stomach' comes from. With saliva also being regarded as non-essential to survival, this is why we sometimes also experience a dry mouth when we are nervous.

An increased urge to use the bathroom is to make the body as light as possible in order to aid in an escape.

In order to produce the amount of energy needed to carry out these functions, our body requires oxygen, which is why we tend to begin breathing rapidly - hyperventilation - into the chest rather than the stomach when we are anxious. The practice of proper breathing technique, which will be discussed later on in the book, can help to prevent this from turning into panic.

Alerted to any possible threats, the body decides that sleep is not an option, lest you become the victim of a predator while at rest. This is why we experience sleepless nights when under stress.

As uncomfortable as these symptoms may be, it is important to note that **they do not cause any harm to you.**

HOWEVER, the mismanagement of them can.

Fear, as part of the fight or flight system, is intended to be a short-term solution I.e. you use the energy it provides to escape from danger, and you calm down not long after when your mind is assured that the danger has passed.

Long-term, we are not designed to constantly experience digestion issues, an increased heartrate and a lack of sleep, without experiencing a litany of physical and mental health issues as a result.

Once again, this is why we need to face our fears head on.

As difficult as this may be, the consequences of not doing it will always outweigh the benefits.

The impact of not facing your fears

As has been stated, fear is ultimately an energy, and as per the first law of thermodynamics, energy cannot be created or destroyed, only converted.

In a situation where we were at genuine risk of serious injury or death, our fear, if used as intended, is ultimately converted into the literal saving of our life.

However, in situations where we **WANT**, **SHOULD** or **NEED** to do something, yet are held back by fear, then that fear will ultimately be converted into **regret** - an infinitely worse feeling than the momentary discomfort caused by fear, and one that will last until said fear has been confronted.

Not facing your fears also results in your mind coming to the conclusion that said fears are justified, and as a result will keep the fight or flight system activated on a constant basis until it determines otherwise.

As your body would not have the energy to have fight-or-flight permanently activated at full intensity, it will instead be operated on a 'short burst' basis.

This means that rather than your mind and body constantly being in the high-intensity state that comes when we're faced with genuine danger, the fight or flight system will operate in short bursts of energy instead, in order to deal with what it deems to be a still-present risk.

This results in a near-constant state of unease and imagining the worst, with physical effects including an upset stomach, restless sleep, and unintended weight fluctuations.

Long-term these can lead to serious health implications, so it is of the utmost importance that they are nipped in the bud. **Your mind and body are effectively producing more of an energy than is required** and facing your fears is the only way to rectify it.

Uncomfortable as it may be, the implications of not doing it are far more serious.

Facing your fears

Now we come to the practical side of fear-management, facing fear head-on, and this begins with your thoughts towards it.

Firstly, as has been mentioned, fear is an energy essential to our survival, and a perfectly healthy emotion, despite the feeling of discomfort that comes with it.

The goal should not be to eliminate fear, for even if this was possible, it would leave you at serious risk of injury or death should you find yourself in a dangerous situation. Instead, **the goal should be to bring your fears down to a manageable level**, one that does not negatively impact your everyday life.

Again, the only way to do this is to face your fears head on.

There is no other alternative to this, it WILL be uncomfortable, and this has to be accepted beforehand.

As daunting as this may be, just remind yourself that **regret is a worse feeling than fear and lasts longer as well**.

Now, we need to clarify what is meant by facing your fears.

As has been discussed, the role of fear is to protect us from danger. Hence, standing in front of a speeding car, or climbing into the enclosure of a dangerous animal, would not count as 'facing your fears', it would count as downright foolishness.

Instead, we should employ the **Want-Should-Need system**.

This is a simple way to determine whether you should do something that scares you, and to implement it, ask yourself three questions

Do I want to do this?

Should I do this?

Do I need to do this?

Simplistic as this system is however, each question needs careful consideration to be answered honestly, which is why this exercise should be done when you have sufficient time to think clearly – not possible once fight or flight is activated - about each one. For maximum clarity, add on the question **"Will I regret not**

doing this?" in order to get the clearest answer to each one.

Though this system and the answers it provides will be unique for everyone, here are a few general examples

WANTS

*You may have feelings towards someone and you **want** to be in a relationship with them. Though you may feel fearful, the best course of action is to simply ask them out. If they say yes, it may develop into a happy relationship. If they say no, though you may be disappointed, you will at least have clarity and you can then move onto someone you're better suited to.*

Not facing your fear of asking them out will leave you asking yourself 'What if?' for a long time.

SHOULDS

*An ad for a new nearby fitness camp comes up in your social media feed. Though you feel that you **should** attend in order to improve your health, none of your friends plan on signing up. Nervous about not knowing anyone, you book a place anyway, and end up not only enjoying it,* *but also developing a new circle of friends who prioritise health & fitness.*

In an alternative version where your fears prevent you from going, you feel a stinging sense of regret when you later see pictures of it on your newsfeed, with all available spaces already filled up.

NEEDS

*Situations where we need to do something, but are prevented from doing so out of fear, thankfully tend to be rare. However, as an example, I will use a bullying co-worker, one who constantly belittles you and fires sniping comments in your direction. With your mental health at risk due to this behaviour, you **need** to take action. Though initially nervous, you eventually pluck up the courage to calmly but assertively tell your co-worker that you don't appreciate their attitude and you expect it to stop. Realising that you're no soft-touch, the bully backs off and the workplace suddenly has a much more pleasurable atmosphere. The bully themselves eventually becomes more pleasurable as well.*

However in a situation where you did not challenge their behaviour out of fear, the bullying continued, and your mental and physical health suffered as a result.

(**Note:** Anger will also have to be controlled in tandem with fear in situations such as above where confrontations arise. I will explain this later on in the book.)

As you can see, each situation shares the common factor where the consequences of not facing a fear, have a far more negative impact than the fear itself, and this risk-reward analysis is an important factor to take into account when you are doing this exercise.

It is also crucial to note that for this system to work, it has to be made into a habit.

As the famous saying goes, *"Do something every day that scares you"*. Every day of our lives we're presented with opportunities to step outside our comfort zones.

Some days we create these opportunities ourselves, other days they create themselves.

Some days, only a mere step outside of our comfort zone is possible, other days it's a leap.

The most important thing is that we take these opportunities, no matter how big or small. In fact, if you don't consistently take the small ones, then you won't be mentally conditioned to take the big ones either.

You won't rise to the occasion, you'll regress to your level of training.

Controlling your thoughts

Now that you've determined what fears you have to face, it's time to use your thoughts to your advantage to mitigate what can be the overwhelming emotional aspects of fear.

As was explained earlier, a key aspect of fear is envisaging the worst case scenario. This is our brain's way of trying to predict future danger so we will be best prepared for it.

Though distressful at times, one of the most effective ways to counter this is to simply ask yourself ***"What's the worst that can happen?"***. A technique so simplistic, that this is perhaps why many disregard its effectiveness.

Once you've answered this question honestly to yourself, you'll find that very rarely will what you're planning on doing have any possible catastrophic consequences.

Again, we'll go back to the situation where you overcome your fear of asking someone you like on a date. Realistically, the worst possible thing that can happen is that they'll say no. Disappointing, yes, but not something that should drastically impact your life in a negative manner.

In fact, as has already been stated, NOT taking the calculated risk of asking them out can actually lead to more negative consequences, such as you constantly wondering 'What if?' to yourself.

Now of course, there are going to be situations where we ask ourselves *"What's the worst that can happen?"*, and we will indeed think of possible situations where we could come to harm.

For example, you're given the opportunity to compete in a White Collar Boxing match. Immediately you envision yourself being brutally knocked out in front of a crowd of your family and friends.

This is where another simple yet effective technique comes into play, simply ask yourself **"What are the chances of it happening?"**.

Yes, as in any Boxing contest, there is the possibility you could be knocked unconscious with one precise blow. However, with the head-guards and oversized gloves that will be used in your bout, the chances of this happening will be reduced dramatically, with stringent health & safety measures put in place to prevent any further damage should it occur.

In fact, with the effort you'll put into training, you'll have an equal, if not more of a chance of knocking out your opponent (who, like you, is also going through the fear response at the prospect of fighting) than they do to you, and even if the outcome of the fight doesn't go your way, your family and friends will recognise the effort you put in to get into the ring in the first place. Anyone who doesn't, is someone whose opinion you should simply not take seriously in the first place.

Realising that the chances of something negative happening are low, and that you are prepared to deal with that situation if it occurs, you take the fight, winning an impressive points decision.

Controlling the physical aspects of fear

As has been explained, the purpose of fear is to remove ourselves as quickly as possible from situations where we are at risk of serious injury or death. In the days where it was the norm to be faced with dangerous predators on your everyday travels, we required an immense amount of energy to quickly escape should we encounter one, lest we ended up as one of their meals.

In the more modern-era, coming face to face with unrestrained carnivorous beasts would not be regarded by most as a common everyday occurrence. However, it is not an impossibility either, I.e. an un-muzzled rabid dog that's gotten off its leash in a local park.

With the brain unable to differentiate between a physical and mental threat, even a university exam or job interview can also trigger the physiological effects of fear, despite there being no physical threat present. Hence the fight or flight system remains, ready to flood your body with adrenaline to aid in any potential escape, should it feel the need has arose.

Therefore, this is why it is crucial to learn how to alleviate what can be the overwhelming physical aspects of fear.

The first way to do this, and perhaps the most simple, is to be conscious of your breathing.

Once fear has been triggered, our bodies require a high volume of oxygen to produce the energy needed to escape from a threat. This results in us breathing rapidly, into our chests rather than our stomachs, which can ultimately result in even more panic.

The technique to rectify this is simple.

With your mouth closed, place the tip of your tongue to the roof of your mouth behind your two front teeth. Breathe in slowly through your nose, into your stomach, for a mental count of four. Hold this breath for a count of seven, then, exhale through pursed lips for a count of eight.

If you feel that these counts don't work, then experiment with what does. Simply inhale through the nose into the stomach **without**

straining yourself to do so, hold without straining yourself, then, exhale through pursed lips, again without strain. The most important thing is to find what works for you.

This exercise results in a steady supply of the oxygen required for the body to operate at an optimum level when under stress, rather than the rapid shallow breathing which quickly results in panic and exhaustion.

It is essential however, that it is practised daily until it becomes a habit that will stay in place when the fight or flight system is activated. Remember, *"You don't rise to the occasion, you regress to your level of training"*.

Thankfully, it is incredibly easy to accomplish this, as it is a technique we can practice as we go about our daily lives. One way to ensure that we are doing it correctly, is to lie flat on our back with a pencil or other light object lying on our stomach, which should expand and contract in unison with our inhalations and exhalations, causing the object to rise.

Summary

Fear is an emotion, that although uncomfortable, is necessary to our survival. To achieve this, it affects us in a number of ways, both mentally and physically.

It is a healthy emotion, it is only when it is mismanaged that it becomes a problem.

To determine whether you should do something that scares you, ask yourself honestly, do you **want** to do it, **should** you do it, and do you **need** to do it? You must then ask yourself *"Will I regret not doing this"* in order to get the most clear answer.

When you've determined what fears you have to face, use the energy your mind and body has produced to face them. This will be difficult. **Not facing them however, will be far more difficult.**

ANGER

Now we come to the second section of the book, the 'fight' component of fight or flight, Anger. An emotion, and an energy, that shares many similarities with fear, but serves a different purpose. Let us begin.

What is Anger?

Let us return to the beginning of the book, as we imagined our caveman ancestor walking through a forest in search of food and other materials. His senses alerted to the nearby rustling of leaves and crackling of branches, he turns around to the sight of a Sabre Tooth Tiger.

However, unlike the first situation where fear allowed your ancestor to quickly escape from becoming a meal of this magnificent beast, the Sabre Tooth Tiger has gotten closer to your stone age relative this time, pouncing on him and pinning him down.

Just as in the first situation, a burst of adrenaline immediately surges through your ancestor's veins and his mind once again switches to a state of intense focus. The difference this time is that his instinct is not to flee, for that opportunity has been rendered impossible, but instead, to fight, with this being the only option available to guarantee his survival.

With the predator not yet sinking its teeth into your ancestor, he seizes the opportunity to grab the Tiger's throat with one hand and strike it repeatedly with the other. His mind, in an intense state of focus on inflicting as much damage as possible, notices a large rock on the ground nearby. Quickly grabbing this, he uses it to strike the Tiger repeatedly, landing on the beast's nose, startling it (ironically this is the Tiger's own fight or flight system at work) and causing it to get off your ancestor and retreat, ultimately allowing your ancestor to survive and reproduce.

Like fear ensuring his survival in the first situation, anger ensured it in this one.

So like Fear, Anger is a good thing as well then?

Yes. As unusual as that sentence sounds, Anger is a perfectly healthy emotion, one that is necessary to prevent our physical and mental boundaries being infringed upon.

Like fear, it is only when this emotion is mishandled that it becomes a problem.

How is anger mishandled?

In the section on fear, I quoted Cus D'Amato, trainer of Mike Tyson, who compared fear to fire.

Like fire, fear is an energy source that once harnessed, can be used to warm your home and cook your meals. If it's not kept under control however, it can cause devastation.

The same principle applies to Anger.

Imagine you work in an office environment that although busy, is managed efficiently. This changes however, with the arrival of a new supervisor.

Similar to the bullying co-worker as envisioned in the section on fear, this supervisor seems to have it in for you, singling you out on numerous occasions in front of other staff members.

Just like fear, your brain cannot differentiate between a physical and mental threat when deciding to activate the anger response. After initially regarding this behaviour as a once-off, your brain begins to detect a pattern, and as a result, the anger response is switched on when you see the supervisor, though in low intensity at first.

As anger is an energy, and energy cannot be created or destroyed, only converted, you let it build up, not knowing how to express it in a healthy manner. This comes to a head when your supervisor once again belittles you in front of your colleagues.

You explode, roaring at the supervisor to f!@k off and squaring up to them. You're suspended on full-pay while an investigation is held. Though you're eventually allowed to return to work following a disciplinary meeting, your chance at promotion is gone. The thought of dismissal during the suspension period became a source of anxiety also, affecting your sleep. You ultimately become unhappy with a job you once looked forward to going to, all because of the mishandling of anger.

The correct way to handle anger

Let us imagine this situation once again, with a different outcome.

You're working in an office environment that although hectic at times, is always managed well through good teamwork. A positive workplace atmosphere is maintained in spite of the high-intensity workload, and you enjoy your job.

The arrival of a new supervisor however, puts this in jeopardy, with them seemingly having a chip on their shoulder towards you.

Having initially disregarded a disparaging comment they made towards you as a once-off, the second time it happens your brain detects a pattern, and knowing that your self-esteem and mental health are at risk, you decide to act.

The following day, when yet another sniping comment is aimed in your direction by your supervisor, you feel your heartbeat begin to increase and your temperature begin to rise as a sudden surge of energy passes through your body.

Rather than explode as in the first situation however, you maintain your deep breathing, remaining fully in control of the powerful emotions that have just been activated. Although nervous, when the opportunity arises to talk to the supervisor on their own, you confidently walk over, maintaining eye contact and **<u>assertively but not aggressively</u>** tell them you don't appreciate the way you're being spoken to, and that you expect it to stop.

Realising that they won't be able to easily get away with trying to bully you, they leave you alone from thereon, and in a twist of irony compared to the first situation, it is the supervisor who is ultimately dismissed for misconduct when they tried their bullying tactics on someone else who ended up reporting them to management. You're promoted to the role of supervisor yourself, and prove very popular amongst other staff members.

A significantly different outcome to the first situation, and one that also illustrates why both fear and anger, ultimately two sides of the same coin, need to be managed together.

The mental aspects of anger

Like fear, anger results in our mind switching to a state of intense focus on a perceived threat, though rather than escaping from this potential danger, you're focused on fighting it instead, with your brain regarding this as being essential to your survival. It is a perfectly healthy emotion that is essential to establish boundaries, though if not managed correctly, can have potentially disastrous consequences.

Anger, like fear, is an energy, and as already discussed, energy cannot be created or destroyed, only converted. **It is ultimately your way of thinking that will decide on what your anger is converted into.**

In the first scenario envisioned in this section, you allowed your anger to build up as a result of a bullying supervisor in work, and with you lacking the knowledge on how to express it in an appropriate and proportionate manner, you exploded, suffering negative consequences as a result. In the second, where you had the knowledge on how to control this powerful emotion, the outcome was far different.

The same emotion was present in both scenarios, **the only difference was your thoughts towards it.**

The healthiest approach to anger is to aim to be **assertive not aggressive,** meaning it should be expressed in a proportionate manner to whatever triggered it in the first place. For example, you're short-changed in a shop by a rude staff member, a situation where you have the right to be angry. Using anger as the fuel that it is however, you assertively demand that you're given the correct change, while also telling that staff member you don't appreciate the way they've spoken to you. You barely raise your voice in this interaction, and your change, and an apology from the staff member are both given to you.

Screaming the shop down however, leads to the police being called, who then usher you outside under threat of arrest. Your money is not returned, and you feel a deep sense of embarrassment and regret at the handling of the situation, despite you initially being in the right.

This again shows why it is crucial that both anger AND fear are managed simultaneously. If someone is making you justifiably angry, then the healthiest approach is to confront them directly about the issue at hand. If you plan on confronting them, then the fear response will likely be activated to some degree. If you're unable to manage the fear response, then you'll be unable to express your anger in a healthy manner, meaning it will eventually be involuntarily expressed in an unhealthy manner instead.

The physical aspects of anger

The physical aspects of anger bear a striking similarity to the physical aspects of fear. Both emotions result in a surge of energy throughout the body, in the case of anger, with the intention of preparing you to physically defend yourself against a threat.

Again, this is crucial why we practice proper breathing technique as outlined in the section on fear. Just as this is essential to prevent us from going into a panic when the fear response is activated, proper breathing can help to prevent us from flying into a rage when anger is activated.

Regular physical activity is also key to helping us regulate both emotions. This can be as simple as a short walk every day. Remember the 1% rule, small consistent improvements will compound over time. If 10,000 steps a day seems out of reach, aim for 8,000 as a starting point instead. If two hours in the gym is overwhelming, begin with half an hour instead.

On this note it's also essential to point out that **anger is a great motivator**. It will unfortunately not always be possible to confront those who have wronged you in a satisfactory manner. Even in the scenario mentioned earlier of confronting a bullying supervisor, a level of tact had to be used i.e. you didn't call them out in front of other staff members lest you be accused of misconduct. However, as the saying goes *"Success is the best revenge"*. Use the excess energy generated to become the best version of yourself, which will include prioritising your physical fitness. This will not only put the emotion to good use, it will eventually have a positive knock-on effect on all areas of your life, from increased confidence, to improved sleep, to more energy.

Take this approach, and you'll very likely end up forgetting about those who wronged you in the first place.

The impact of not managing anger

In the section on fear, it was outlined that although controlling fear was not an easy task, the long-term effects of NOT controlling it proved far more serious. The same principle applies to anger.

You may be uneasy at the idea of becoming more assertive. You may think you'll be seen as 'difficult' or 'confrontational'. However, regardless of your view, the anger generated will eventually manifest itself in one form or another. It is your way of thinking that will determine whether this will be through a difficult but necessary conversation with a family member, friend or co-worker regarding the overstepping of a boundary; a conversation where although you're aggrieved, you remain calm as you explain your view.

Alternatively, you allow your anger to build up instead, before you eventually explode at the slightest inconvenience.

On this note, it is important to note that like fear, regret is also linked with the mishandling of anger, whereas **not controlling your fear can prevent you from doing things that you'll regret not doing, not controlling your anger can cause you to do things that you'll regret doing.**

For example, we'll go back to the first scenario of lashing out at a bullying supervisor in work. Though the emotion was justified, it was expressed in an entirely disproportionate manner, leading to you being suspended from work and losing out on the prospect of promotion, something you end up regretting. Another widespread example is saying something hurtful to a loved one 'in the heat of the moment', which can leave us racked with guilt.

Like fear, the mismanagement of anger can also lead to an array of physical health complications, owing to the fight or flight system operating on a constant basis. These can include negatively impacted sleep patterns and hypertension. Mentally, repression of anger can lead to feeling sullen and irritable. As Sigmund

Freud said *"Depression is anger turned inwards"*.

Again, like fear, managing anger will sometimes be difficult. **Not managing it however, will be far more difficult.**

Summary

Anger, like fear, is a perfectly healthy emotion that is essential to establish emotional and physical boundaries. It is only when it is mismanaged that it becomes an issue.

The aim towards anger should not be to get rid of it, for like fear, if this was possible it would leave you at great risk. It should be to have it a manageable level. You should aim to be assertive, not aggressive.

This means your anger must be expressed in a proportionate manner to whatever activated it in the first place.

This means you will have to be willing to stand up to those who knowingly or unknowingly cross your boundaries. This is also why it is essential to learn how to control fear in unison with anger, as it's likely that confrontation will trigger the fear response to some degree.

It will not always be possible to confront those who have wronged you in a satisfactory manner however, **so other outlets will have to be developed in order to process the energy your mind & body has created**. As we come to the final section of the book, I will now go into detail on what I believe is the most effective outlet for the powerful emotions of fear and anger – the sport of Boxing.

BOXING

" A harmless man is not a good man.

A good man is a very, very dangerous man who has that under voluntary control." **– Dr Jordan B Peterson**

Why the sport of Boxing in particular?

Perhaps the most instinctual response when we have been angered to a certain degree, is to curl up our fists in preparation to strike whatever, our whoever, has caused us to be angry in the first place. Even in infant toddlers, this can be seen during temper tantrums when they clench their fists and bang the ground.

However, as much as it necessary to **maintain your composure whilst angered, and not lash out**, it is a stark reality of the world that evil people exist, and this subsequently ensures the likelihood that at some point in our lives, to prevent ourselves or a loved one becoming the victim of a serious assault by said evil people, defending ourselves physically **WILL** be the proportionate response.

Therefore, to fully harness our fight or flight system, it is crucial that we learn how to throw a punch with proper technique, lest we deliver a defensive blow to a potential attacker that is not only ineffective, but also results in injury to our hand or wrist.

There is no more effective sport to learn this technique than Boxing, and the famed 1-2 straight punch combination.

Do not take this as me being dismissive of other combat sports however. I am merely speaking from my own personal experience from training in both martial arts and Boxing. As Boxing has personally been the most effective for me in learning how to control fear and anger, and developing self-confidence, it is the example I've chosen for this book.

If Boxing is not your personal preference then other forms of combat I would recommend are MMA, Muay Thai, Kickboxing and Krav Maga. The most important factor being that they have a striking element involving the fist and/or a live sparring component in training.

Remember, if you're not a good person who is capable of violence, then you'll be left at the mercy of an evil person who is.

How can Boxing help with fear?

First, let's imagine a scenario. Using the lessons learned from this book, you've brushed any nerves aside and joined your local Boxing club. You're willing to step out of your comfort zone and challenge yourself physically and mentally, and meet new people in the process. This is an achievement in itself, and you should be proud.

Next, as the training gets underway, you get ready for sparring. Again, this is a step out of your comfort zone. Though an essential form of training, sparring is still a fight, and willingly choosing to engage in physical combat with another person is a choice that most people would avoid, due to the mental pressure involved and risk of injury. Having read this book and applied its lessons however, you are able to handle the emotion of fear that arises (rest assured, the very same emotion is present in your sparring partner) and give a good account of yourself despite your inexperience. Your confidence rises.

As a result, you're picked to compete on an upcoming show. Though there are some similarities between a real bout and sparring, there are key differences also. The gloves are lighter, and the intention is to win the fight, not to practice for one as is the purpose of sparring. The inclusion of fighting in front of a crowd of people, likely including your friends and family, is another added pressure also.

Nevertheless, having applied the lessons learned in this book on how to handle fear, listened to your coaches, and trained hard, you impressively win the fight after the referee issues a second standing eight count to your opponent in the second round. This came as a result of you repetitively drilling the 1-2 straight punch combination in shadowboxing, a crucial training technique to help sharpen your muscle memory for a fight, when making conscious decisions on what strategies to employ can prove difficult, owing to fight or flight and the release of adrenaline.

The above scenario is a very broad description of what may happen in your Boxing journey should you put the effort in. It may not be the experience of everyone. Whatever your experience in Boxing training and fighting may be however, there are lessons on managing fear that you can take from it that can be applied universally.

For example, it's fight night. Your physical conditioning is on point, you've imagined all possible situations that could play out and practiced your responses through visualisation and shadowboxing, and although nerves are present, you have them completely under control. Despite all this, you come up against a naturally more talented opponent and lose on points. Something similar could also occur in sparring if your partner is again just simply more gifted.

There is absolutely no shame in this whatsoever. In fact, there's actually quite a lot to be proud of.

In a world where many people lead unfulfilled lives, afraid to step out of their comfort zones for fear of what other people may think, you took what could be argued is one of the biggest calculated risks out there. You chose to get into a Boxing ring with a person of similar weight and experience level, and exchange blows in front of a crowd of your peers.

Win, lose or draw, you've just done something that many people could only dream of. You've also gained something else that sets you apart from the majority, the ability to physically defend yourself.

Maintain this mind-set, and there should be very little in life that will faze you.

How can Boxing help with Anger?

As has just been mentioned, subconsciously knowing that you are capable of defending yourself is a massive confidence booster. Although you feel fear whenever you step out of your comfort zone, not only do the lessons learned from this book help you mitigate the physical and mental effects, knowing in the back of your mind that you possess the ability to physically defend yourself should a threat arise, sets you at ease also.

Psychologically, this also has a similar effect on anger.

Imagine, you lack the self-confidence to stand up for yourself and as a result, you go through life browbeaten and disrespected by your peers. Your brain, correctly classifying the unhappiness that arises from this as a threat to your wellbeing, decides that anger needs to be generated in order to bring about change.

However, as you lack the confidence to express this anger in an assertive manner, you have no choice but to repress it instead. As a result, your unhappiness is compounded even further, and your physical health is also affected through high blood pressure and disturbed sleep patterns arising from a constant sullen mood. You are prone to occasionally losing your temper and lashing out also.

Developing the ability to defend yourself however, turns out to be a game-changer.

Knowing in the back of your mind that you are capable of throwing a quick and devastating punch, you are subconsciously reassured that you will be able to handle yourself in a worst-case scenario situation such as being the target of an unprovoked assault.

You also become acutely aware that in difficult but necessary confrontations where your boundaries have been overstepped and you need to assert yourself, should the other party become aggressive and seek to escalate by physically attacking you, you are more than capable of defending yourself.

As a result, you develop the self-confidence to express your anger in an assertive manner whenever your boundaries have been crossed. Any excess energy generated is also regulated through the healthy physical outlet that Boxing provides for.

Summary

Fear and anger, though both serving different purposes, also bear some similarities on a physiological level.

Both emotions result in a surge of energy throughout the body. Boxing, a high-intensity sport, provides the perfect outlet for this energy.

On a psychological level, our thoughts towards fear and anger can exacerbate their effects. The confidence that arises from Boxing training however, can do the exact opposite.

Conclusion

As we reach the end of the book, I hope that you have taken something from it that brings benefit to your life. Whether it be learning to control one of the emotions discussed that you may have had difficulty with, or both, or developing an interest in Boxing and physical fitness, I am confident that my work will have something in it to benefit all who read it.

I would also like to reiterate what I said in the introduction. For this book to have any impact on the reader, the lessons learned will have to be applied in your life on a daily basis. This will be difficult, but it will also be very much worth it as well.

Best of luck in whatever your journey may be.